Dot Marker
Animal Adventure

by Happy Kids Press

A turkey gobbling in a field

A stingray gliding through the water

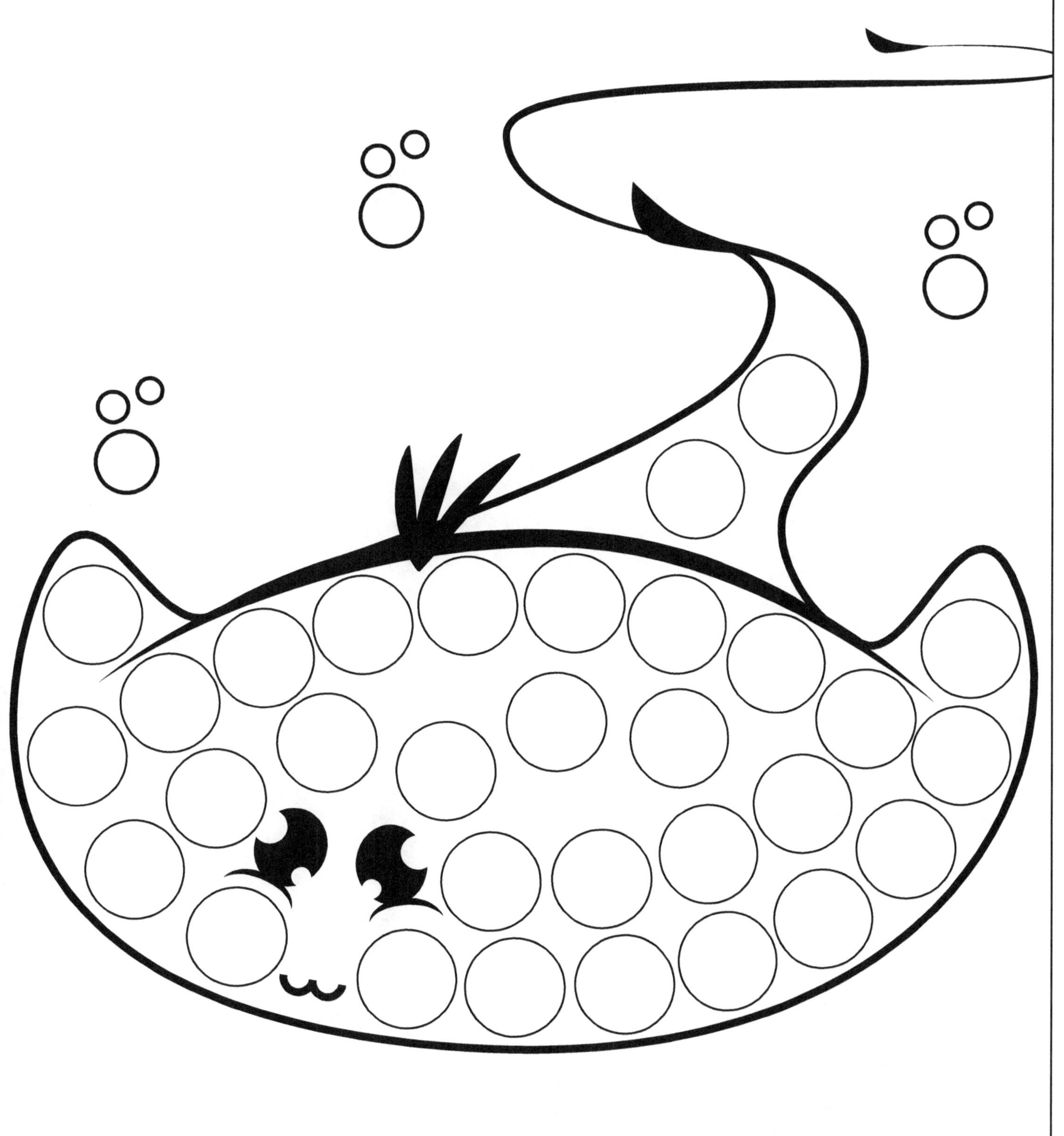

A zebra grazing on grass

A frog jumping from lily pad to lily pad

A lamb frolicking in a field

A skunk waddling along

A clownfish hiding in an anemone

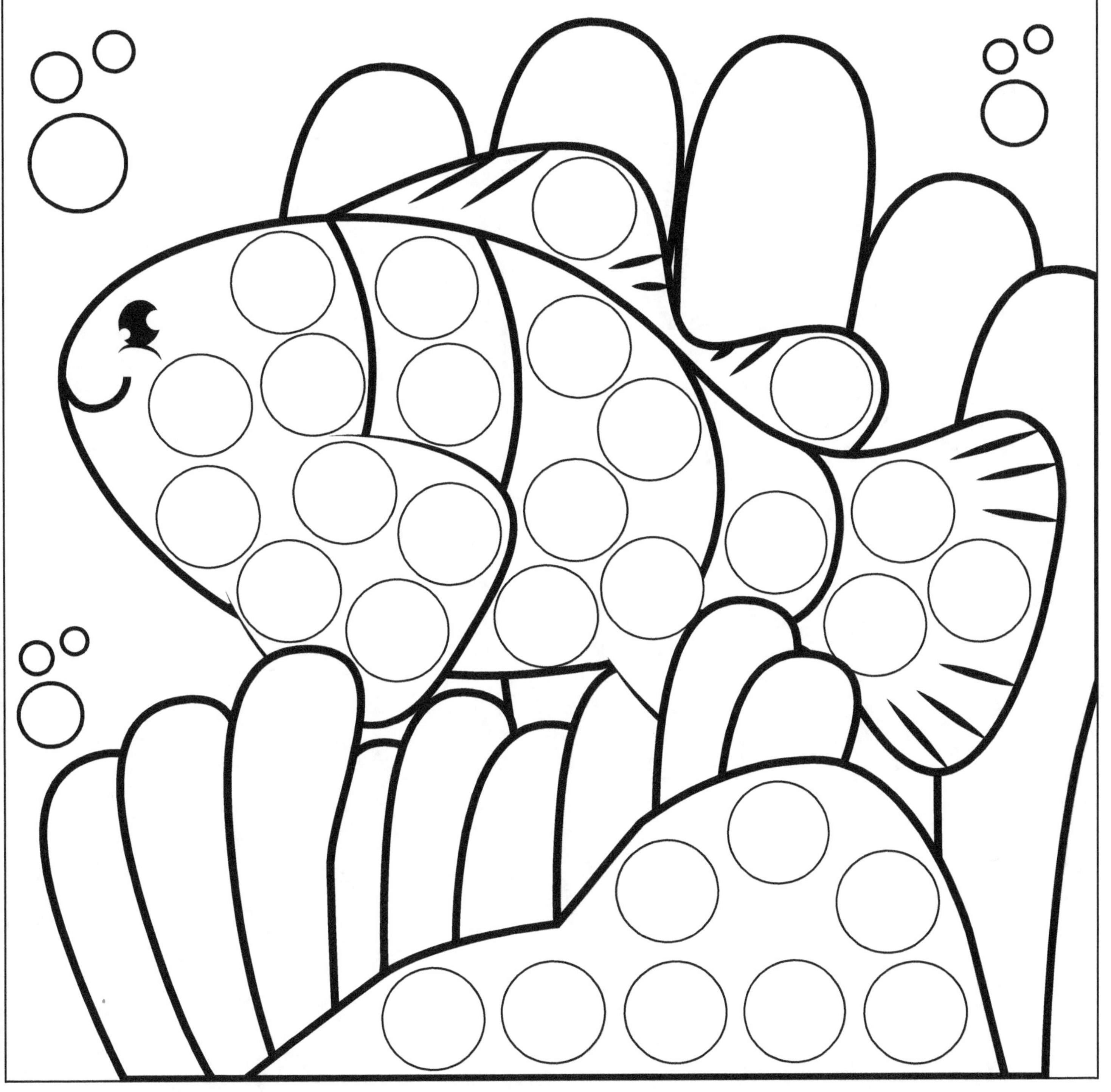

A lion napping in the sun

A lion napping in the sun

A bee buzzing around a hive

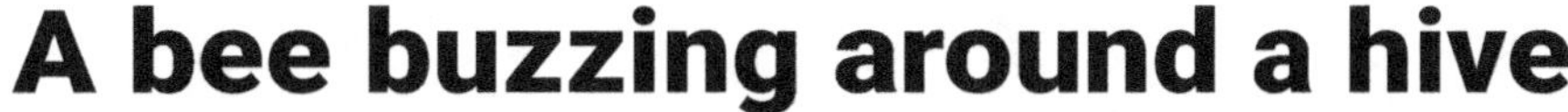

A hedgehog rolling into a ball

A chipmunk stuffing its cheeks with nuts

A shark swimming in the ocean

A pelican diving for fish

A horse grazing in a meadow

A koala cuddled up in a tree

A bumblebee pollinating a flower

A starfish clinging to a rock

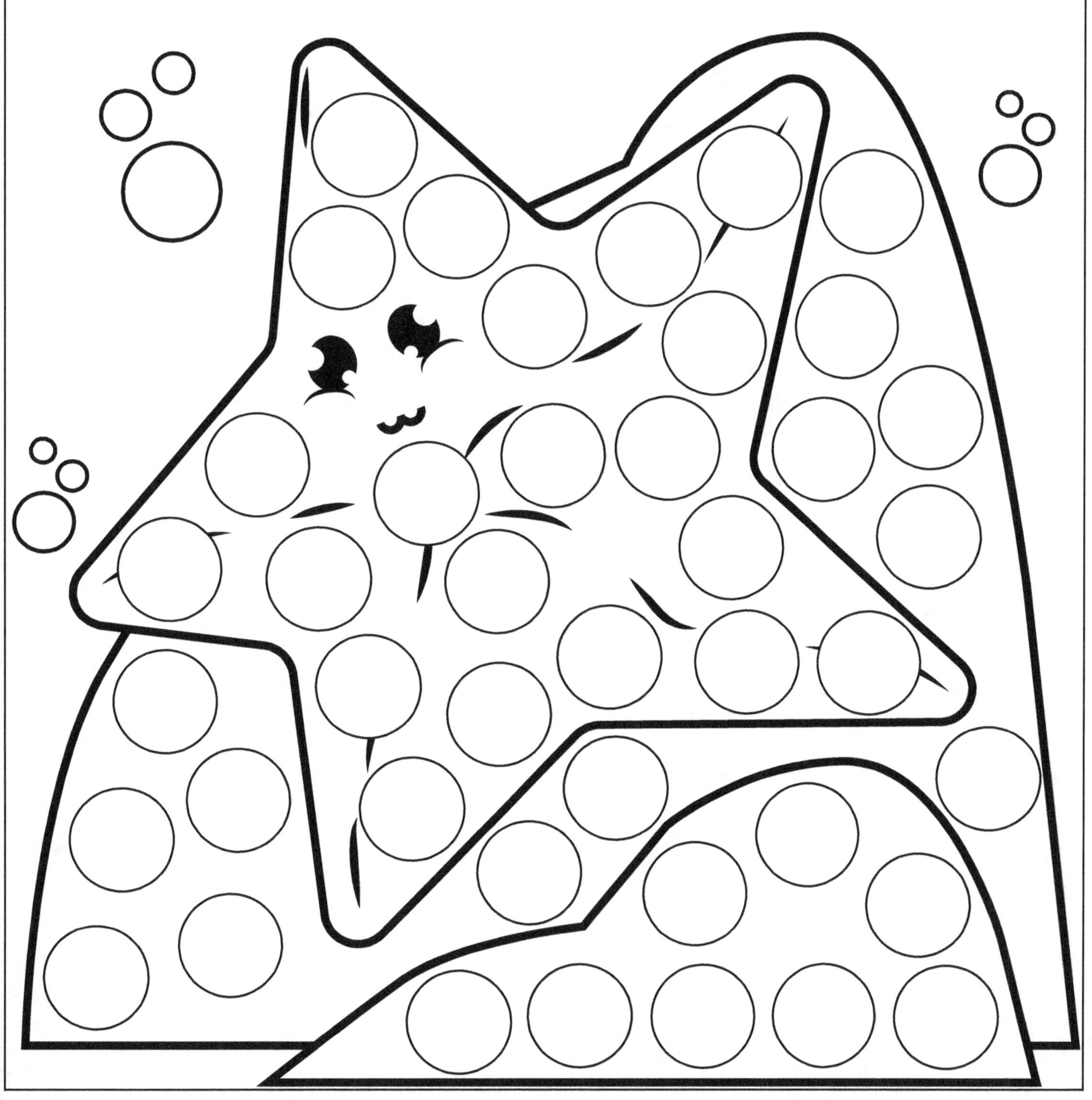

A seagull flying over the ocean

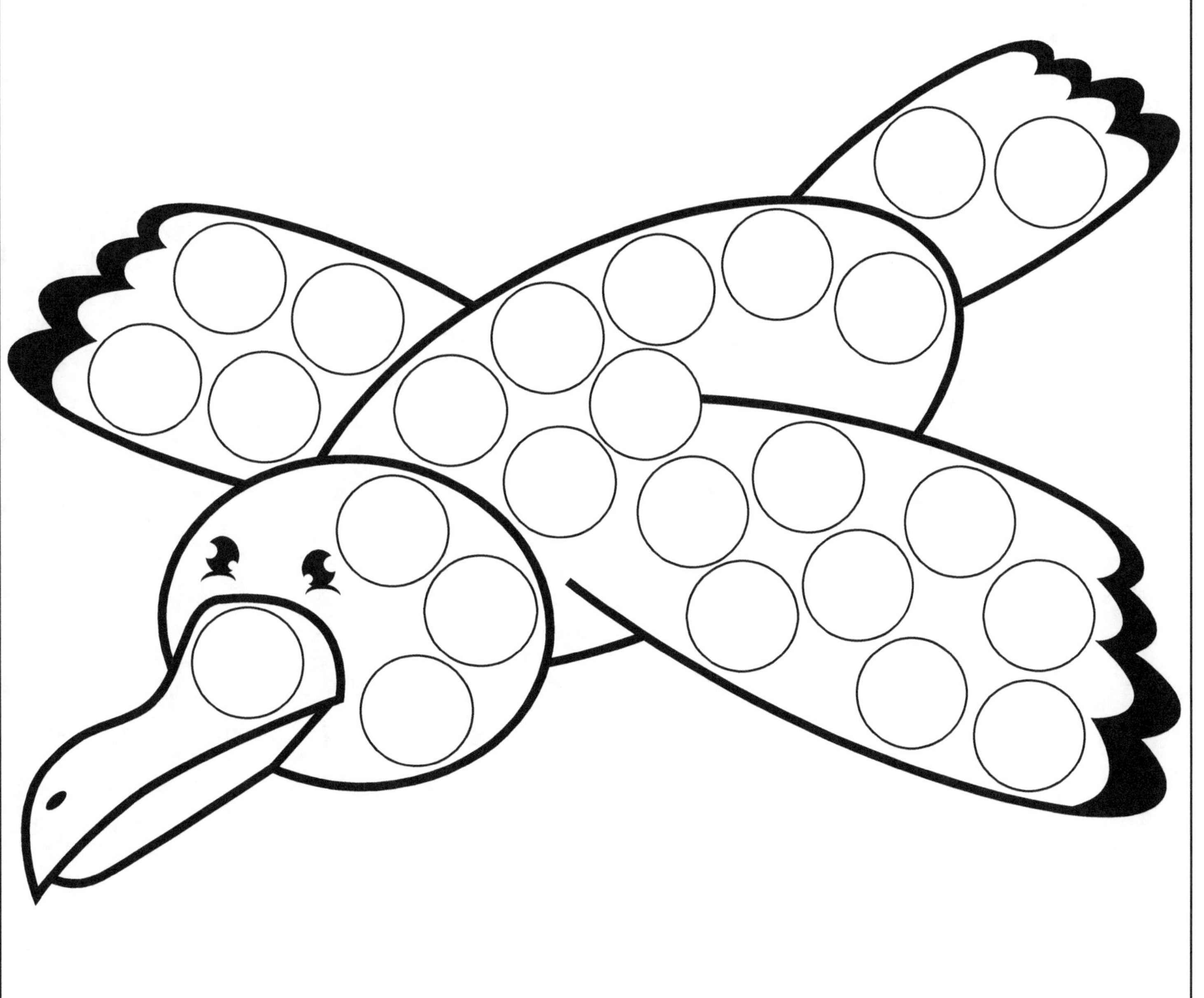

A squirrel collecting acorns

A monkey swinging from a tree branch

A meerkat standing up on hind legs

A jellyfish floating in the water

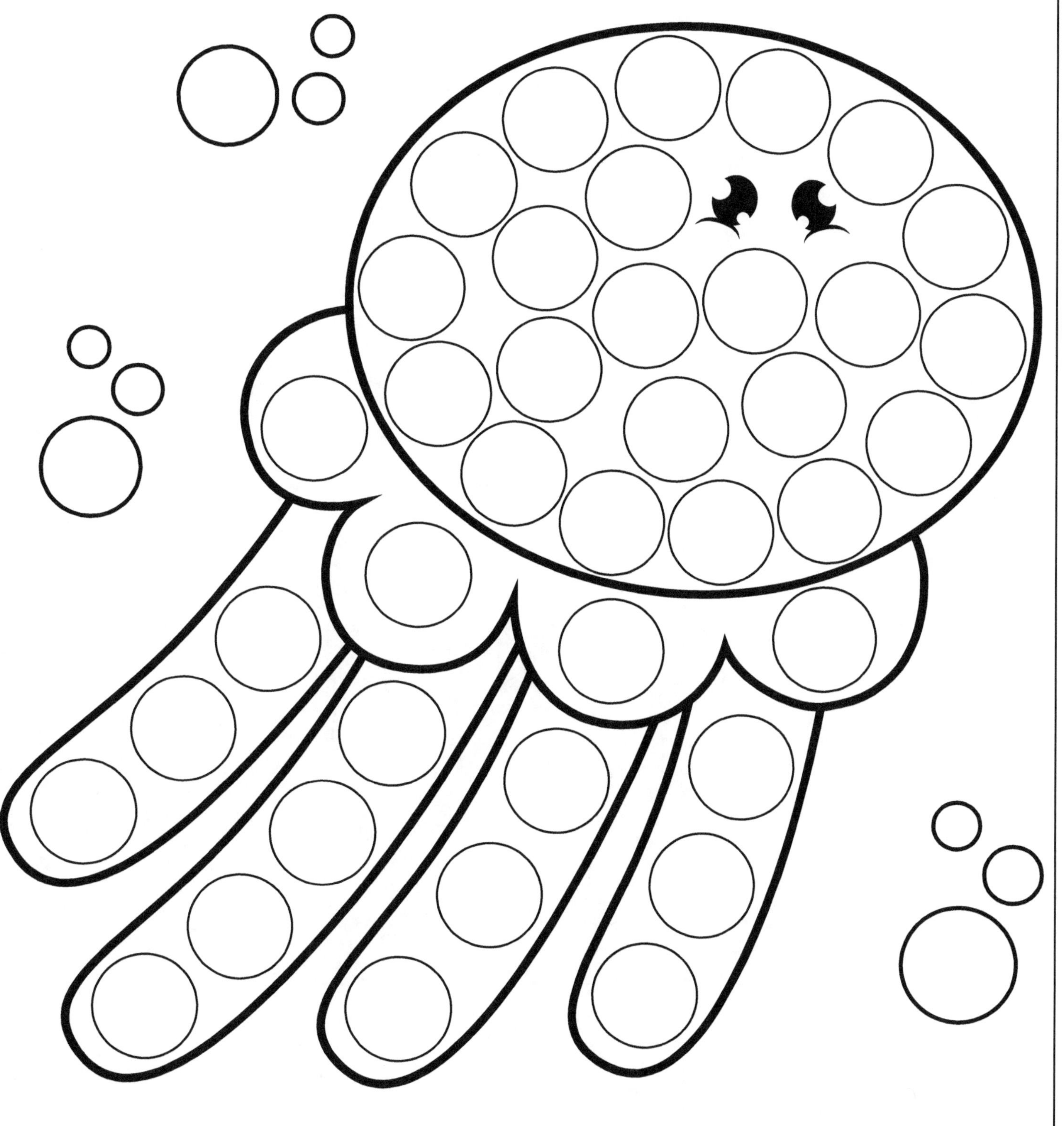

A parrot perched on a branch

A flamingo standing on one leg

A duckling swimming in a pond

A flamingo family

An octopus squirting ink

A kangaroo with a joey in her pouch

A panda eating bamboo

A bunny eating a carrot

A cheetah sprinting across the savannah

A lobster hiding in a rock crevice

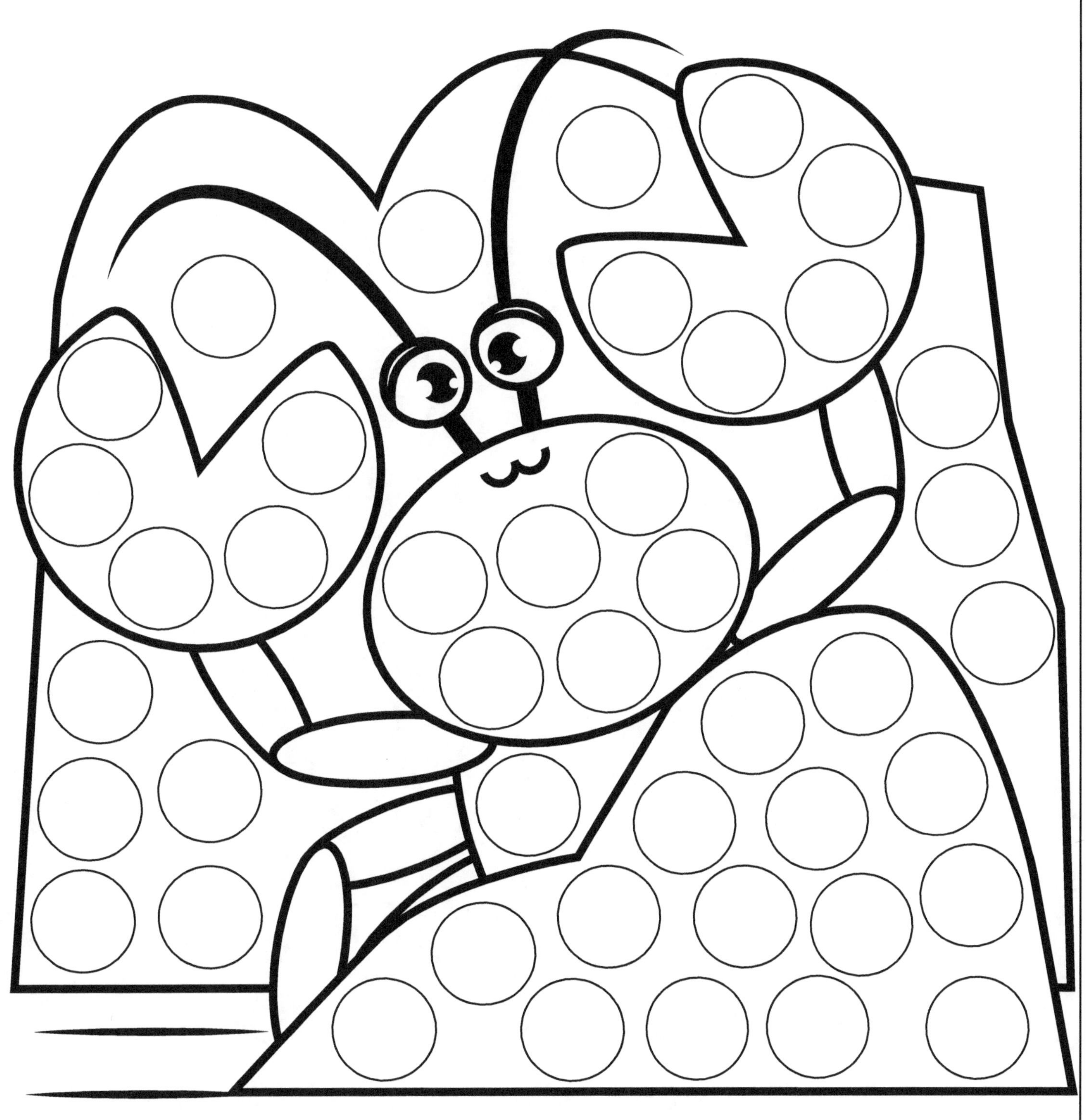

A giraffe reaching for leaves on a tree

A turtle sunbathing on a rock

A baby chick hatching from an egg

A rhinoceros grazing on grass

A crab scuttling across the beach

A dolphin jumping out of the water

A ladybug crawling on a blade of grass

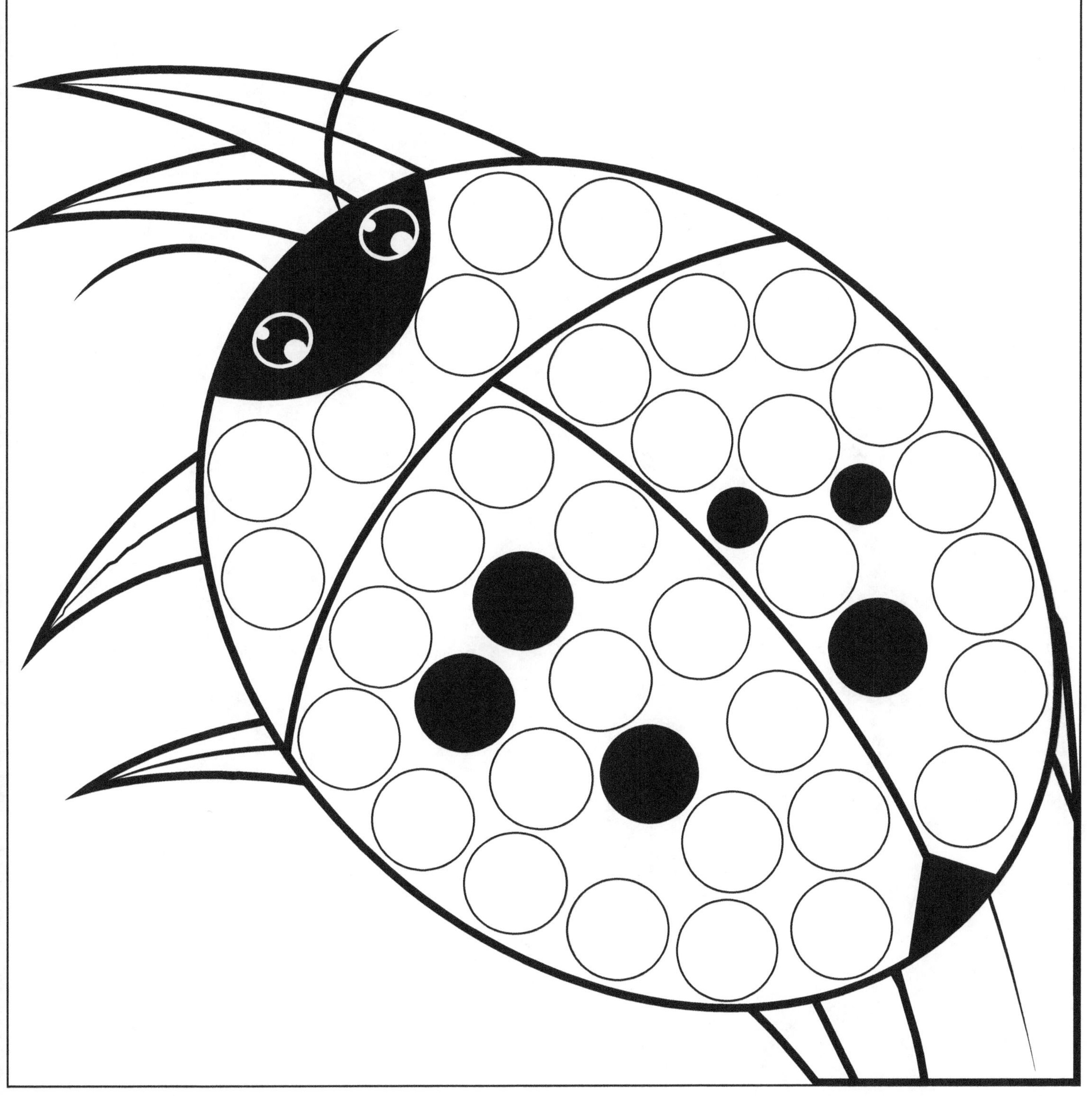

A puppy taking a nap

A crocodile basking in the sun

A whale breaching in the ocean

A penguin waddling on ice

A snail inching along a leaf

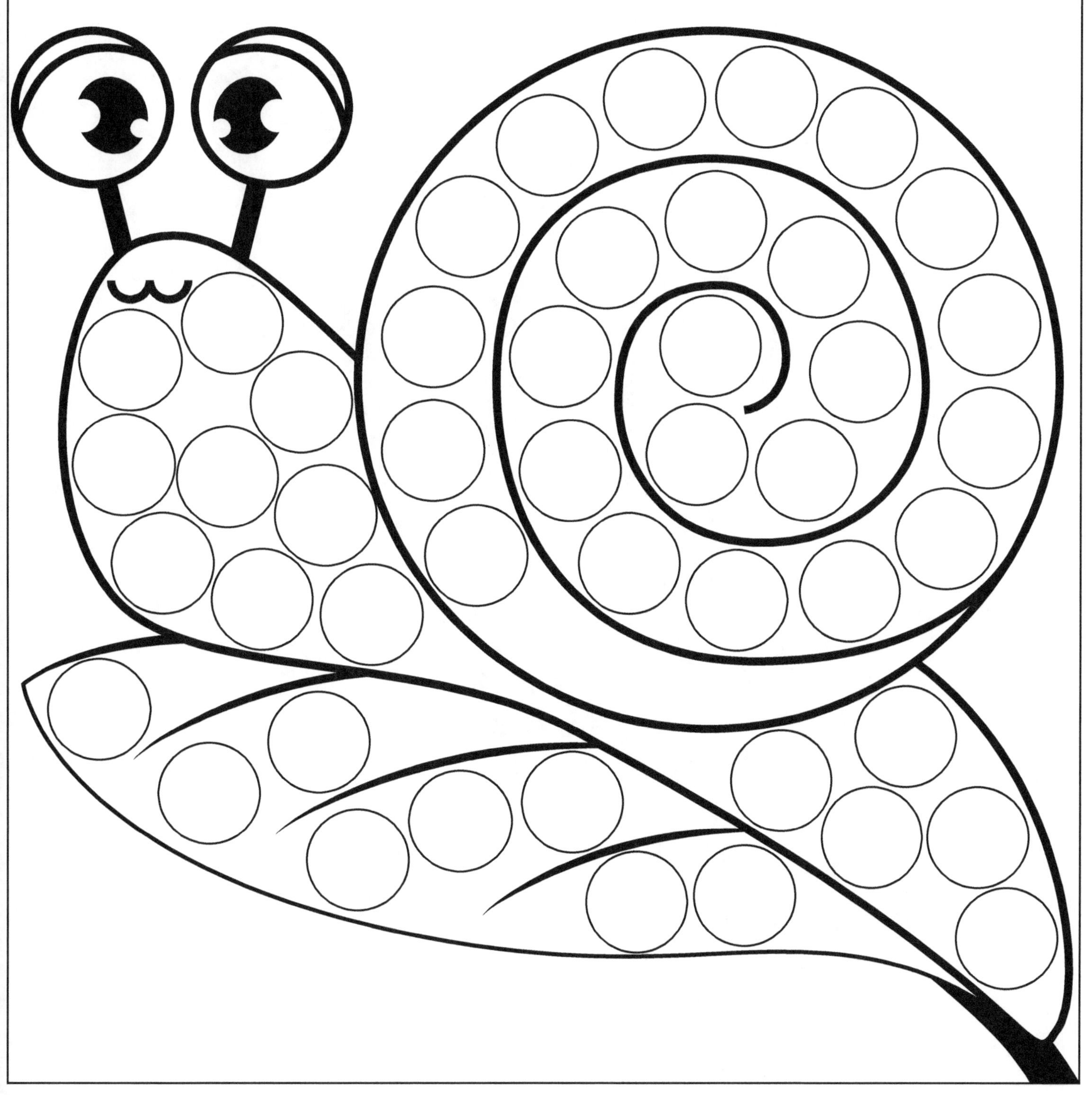

A kitten playing with a ball of yarn

A rooster crowing at sunrise

A seahorse clinging to seaweed

A deer drinking from a stream

A bear fishing in a stream

A butterfly landing on a flower